RAIN FOREST

HELEN COWCHER

André Deutsch Children's Books
Scholastic Children's Books
London

Many creatures dwell in the rain forest. There are sloths, tapirs, anteaters, and Blue Morpho butterflies.

Toucans, macaws, and monkeys live in the forest canopy. There is plenty of food and water for all the creatures, whether they make their home in the trees or on the ground.

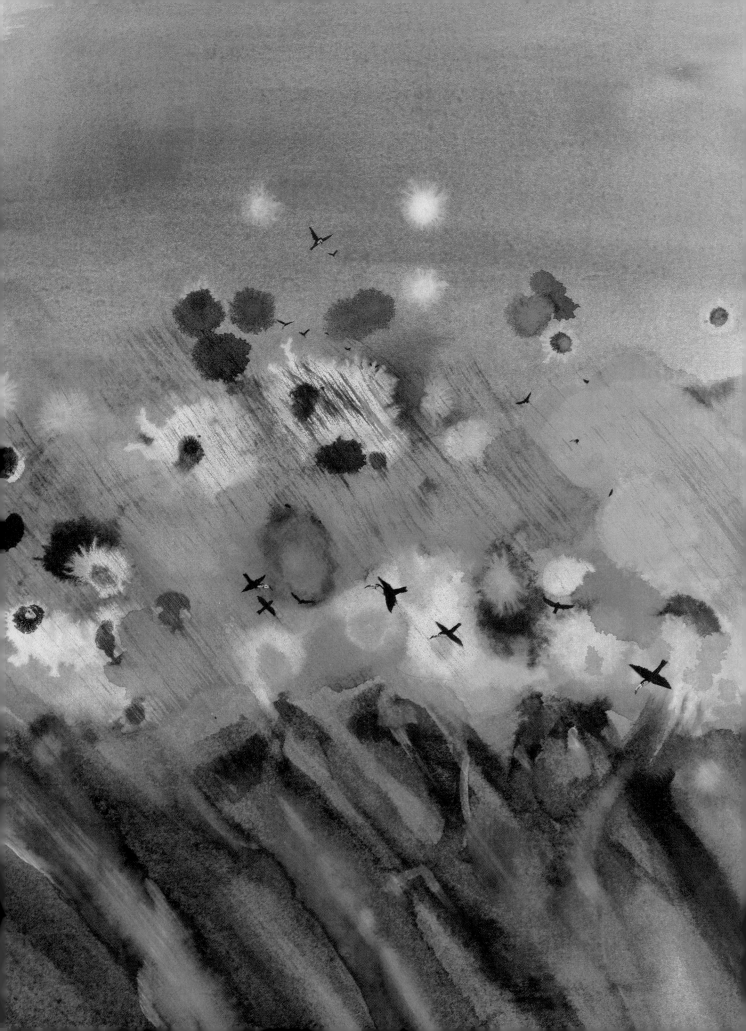

One day, the forest stirred.

From afar, there came a terrible tale.

The birds had lost their perches. All the trees were falling down!

Toucan heard this message with deep foreboding.

Sloth also was worried. He felt rumblings in the forest.

A strange scent floated on the wind, causing the Blue Morpho butterflies to flutter higher among the treetops. The macaws, too, sensed something sinister in the air.

The anteaters stopped foraging
and crept into the undergrowth.

Tapirs trooped off into the shadows.

Howler monkey screeched a warning to his
fellows. They heard him miles away.

Jaguar roared with fury and sped through the trees. The animals shuddered. Jaguar was the most powerful creature in the rain forest.

But something even more powerful was
threatening their world.

Machines!
Cutting and spoiling!

Jaguar heard a voice.
"Go to high ground,"
it said.
"Go to high ground."

The rains came as the animals made their way
higher and higher. Fear drove them on.

Then the floods came! There were no trees to
hold the soil in place, so the river burst its banks.
The Machine was washed away!

But the creatures of the rain forest were safe.

The animals looked down on the swirling water, the broken tree trunks, and the muddy banks, and they wondered how long the tall trees would be there to guard them.